Glass Painting

By Diana Fisher

The author and publisher would like to express their gratitude
to Pébéo, and Angela Scherz in particular,
for their generous gifts of time and supplies.

Walter Foster Publishing, Inc.
23062 La Cadena Drive
Laguna Hills, CA 92653
www.walterfoster.com

Contents

Introduction 3

Gathering Your Materials 4

Getting Prepared 6

Mastering Basic Techniques 8

Suncatchers: Working with Outliners 10
    Suncatcher Templates 12

Painted Fishbowl: Sponging on a Curved Surface 14
    Fishbowl Templates 19

Pasta Canister: Merging and Blending Paints 20
    Pasta Canister Templates 24

Beaded Perfume Bottle: Embellishing with Glass Beads 25
    Perfume Bottle Template 29

Olive Oil Bottle: Painting on Glass Jewels 30

Pedestal Fruit Bowl: Glass Painting with Markers 34
    Fruit Bowl Templates 39

Floral-Patterned Plate: Opaque Layering with Drybrush 40
    Floral Plate Template 43

Wedding Flutes: The Etched-Glass Look .44
    Wedding Flutes Templates 47

Holiday Ornaments: Painting with Applicator Bottles 48
    Holiday Ornaments Templates 51

Whimsical Mirror: Stenciling 52
    Whimsical Mirror Templates 55

Colorful Candlesticks: Doing a Flat Wash 56

Peacock Vase: Using an Angled Brush 58
    Peacock Vase Templates 63

More Great Glass Painting Ideas: The Next Step 64

Introduction

The beauty of stained glass has been capturing imaginations since the first medieval artists created cathedral windows. Until recently, colored glass creations involved specialized training and equipment. Now there is a new generation of easy-to-use glass paints available that produce lasting works of art with the same vivid, lustrous colors you find in stained glass.

In this book, I will show you in detail how to create your own stunning pieces in a variety of styles and techniques. For each project, I present clear, step-by-step instructions and offer helpful tips that will make glass painting easy to learn and fun to explore. And because mistakes are easily washed off, success is virtually guaranteed. I even provide templates and stencils for most projects, so you needn't possess any special artistic skills. However, once you get started, I think you'll find yourself brimming with ideas for transforming plain glass jars and bottles into richly painted heirlooms to treasure. So scan your kitchen for that unique jam jar, and let's get started!

Gathering Your Materials

All of the supplies you will need can be easily found at your local craft store; some you may already have at home. Although I illustrate an array of options, you can begin with just a few basics: a glass jar or bottle, glass paints and thinner, a palette for mixing the paints, a few small round brushes and one large flat one, sponges, and a plastic squirt bottle.

Choosing Your Glass

You may use any piece of ordinary glass or crystal you like. Look for interesting items in craft, import, and department stores; antique shops; specialty kitchen boutiques; and even grocery stores. You may also want to comb secondhand shops for unusual, and often inexpensive, pieces.

Picking Your Paints

There are a number of glass paints available. I use water-based thermo-hardening glass paints, outliners, and markers. They are non-toxic and clean up beautifully with water, so there's no need for harsh solvents. Best of all, the colors are made permanent by baking the painted piece in an ordinary kitchen oven.

Decorative Glass Because most of the glass paints are transparent, I chose clear glass items for the projects in this book. But don't limit yourself. You may be inspired by a cobalt blue bowl that would look lovely with a silver scroll.

Whatever the line of glass paints you've chosen, it should include a diluting agent, or thinner. Thinners are used to make the paint flow more evenly and to extend the drying time. Don't substitute water for thinner, however; water will weaken the thermo-hardening properties of the paints.

Using Applicators

Soft brushes, such as watercolor brushes, are best for glass paints. To start, you'll need one wide, flat brush for covering large areas and for blending. You'll also need one small, one medium, and one large round brush for painting decorations and filling in outlines. You'll find a large range of choices at craft and art supply stores.

Glass Paints Here are some of the outliners, jars, and markers of glass paints I use. They include not only the glossy colors and mediums most commonly seen in glass painting, but also the frosted colors and mediums that create an etched-glass look and an iridescent medium that produces a pearl finish.

Sponges are great for achieving textured finishes. Finely grained sponges such as the ones shown in the photo at right can be purchased at craft stores. Of course, you can also use sea sponges or even plain kitchen sponges, but bear in mind that they will yield a coarser texture.

Another method of applying paint is to use plastic squeeze bottles to squirt paint onto the glass surface, letting the colors run, merge, and flatten. This creates a brilliant finish. Craft stores carry such applicator bottles, but you can also use plastic hair-coloring bottles. (If you recycle used hair-dye bottles, just make sure you clean them out thoroughly first!)

Palettes and Applicators I apply paints from jars with either brushes, sponges, or squeeze bottles, depending on the effect I want to achieve. I also use both palettes and small jars or recycled food cans for mixing my colors before I apply them to the glass.

Homemade Palette Plastic wrap stretched over a plate makes an instant, no-fuss palette in a pinch.

Selecting a Palette

Palettes come in all shapes, sizes, and materials. Ceramic and metal palettes can be washed out with water and reused. However, glass paints won't wash off plastic palettes well, so you'll have to throw those palettes away after use. Some palettes come with plastic covers, which are great for keeping your mixed paints from drying up between painting sessions. And don't forget to keep some small dishes on hand for mixing large amounts of paint that your palette can't manage.

Assembling the Extras

You may want to make the following additions to your list of basic materials. Use a transparent jar of water for rinsing your brushes between colors; you'll be able to see when the water needs changing. Keep rubbing alcohol on hand to degrease the glass surface before painting it; use cotton pads or lint-free paper towels as applicators. Cotton swabs work well for cleaning up the edges of your painted image, and a craft knife or utility knife can be used to scrape off unwanted paint and to cut out stencils. Newspaper or white paper will protect your work surface, and masking tape will hold your templates in place and mask off areas you want to keep free of paint.

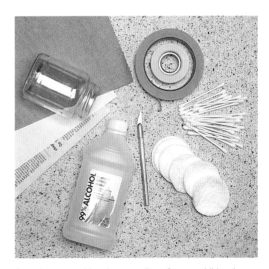

Supplements Here is a sampling of some additional materials you'll find handy for glass painting. I will mention other useful tools I've discovered as they come up in the individual projects.

Getting Prepared

Setting Up Your Work Station

Any small space will do for a work area, but you'll want to find a flat surface in a well-lit and well-ventilated area. It's also a good idea to cover the surface with newsprint or white paper to protect it from spills. I prefer using white paper; it provides a plain background for the clear glass, making it easy to see any paint spills that might mar the piece I'm working on. Newspaper end rolls can be purchased very cheaply, and they're perfect for this purpose.

My Work Area My favorite work surface is my kitchen table, securely covered with plain, white paper.

Cleaning the Glass

Oils and dirt can interfere with the glass paint's ability to adhere to the surface, so before you begin painting, it's important to clean your glass pieces in soapy water and then degrease them with rubbing alcohol. You can remove tough stains on hard-to-reach areas (such as inside narrow-necked bottles) with denture cleaner dissolved in hot water. To remove residual adhesive from labels, try rubbing with a cotton pad wetted with nail polish remover.

Preparing the Surface To clean the glass, I use a little rubbing alcohol on a cotton pad; then I wipe the surface with a lint-free paper towel to remove any leftover fibers.

Washing Off Mistakes

Water-based thermo-hardening glass paints are water-soluble until baked, which means that whatever you're not completely satisfied with can be removed with water before baking. Small mistakes can be lifted off with a wet cotton swab, and a whole design can be rinsed off under running water. If the paint has been on the glass for several hours, first soak the glass in warm water for a few minutes, and then rinse.

Starting Over Don't worry; everyone makes mistakes. When I need to remove large areas of paint, I rinse the entire piece in my kitchen sink.

Baking Your Creation

Baking requirements vary among the different paints—and some don't require baking at all—so be sure to follow the directions for the specific paints you buy. The paints I use in this book call for 24 hours (48 hours for outliners) of drying time before being placed in the oven. If the paint is very thick or the air is very humid, the piece may need to air-dry for longer than the recommended time. After the piece has air-dried, I place it in a cold oven with the temperature set at 325°F (160°C), wait until the oven reaches the temperature, and then set the timer for 40 minutes. After the glass has baked for 40 minutes, I turn the oven off and let the glass cool completely before removing it from the oven. And voilà—my colored glass creation is ready to use!

Once baked, the paints I use are both microwave-safe and dishwasher-safe, and because they are nontoxic, they can safely come into contact with food. This isn't true for all types of glass paints, so be sure to check the labels carefully. **And do note that although you can bake a piece more than once (between layers or steps), you should not bake it more than three times in total.**

Setting the Paints One of the conveniences of thermo-hardening glass paints is that they don't need extremely high temperatures for curing, so you can bake them in your own home oven.

Mastering Basic Techniques

Before you begin a project, it's a good idea to practice a few basic painting techniques. This will help you get a "feel" for the paints—how they flow and what kind of coverage you get—so you can paint with confidence. Don't be afraid to experiment. Remember: you can always wash off the paints with tap water!

Mixing Colors The glossy glass paints are transparent, exhibiting a luster that perfectly complements glass. The colors also mix well and do not become "muddy," as other paints such as acrylics do. You can create a wide range of colors by mixing them together on your palette.

Blending Glass paints can also be mixed directly on the glass itself by layering colors. Painting a layer on top of another wet layer is called "painting wet-on-wet." You can blend the colors completely for a solid hue or let the separate strokes of colors show, creating a "rainbow" effect.

Dry Layering You can create a different kind of blend by baking the piece or letting the paint air-dry between layers. This technique is best for precise designs, where you want to control exactly how and where the colors blend together.

Painting a Wash Washes are a great way to quickly apply color to large areas. To make a wash, first add thinner to the color. Begin with a few drops of solution, and gradually add more until you get the consistency you want. Then apply a generous amount of paint to the glass with a flat brush, always stroking in the same direction.

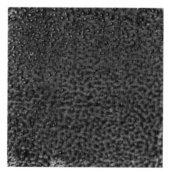

Sponging for Texture Sponges are wonderful tools for creating texture, and sponging is another way to quickly apply color to the glass. Dip the sponge in the paint and wipe off the excess on the edge of a dish or paper towel before dabbing color on the glass. Test this technique on a practice piece or a sheet of plastic wrap to see the effects you can get.

Blending with Sponges Sponges can also be used as a blending tool, particularly if you want a mottled look. Simply dab on a layer of color, and then sponge a second color over the first. You can cover the first layer completely, or leave some areas un-layered for a less perfect blend. Try using both fine sponges and coarsely textured sponges for different effects.

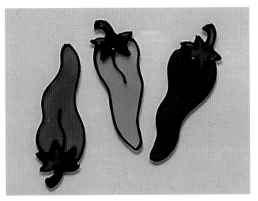

Outlining To achieve the look of stained glass, I use a black outliner to trace the lines of my design first. Once the lines have dried, I paint the color into each section with a small round brush. Outliners can be a little tricky to control, so you might want to practice on a sheet of paper or plastic to get a feel for the medium, before you try it on a curved glass surface.

One-Stroke Painting Flower petals and leaves can be painted in one stroke, pressing down for thick spots and lifting the brush for thinner areas. Work toward the middle of each flower or leaf, tapering off the petal at its midpoint and tapering off the leaf at the stem. In the example here, I used a sponge for the centers of some of the flowers and added accents with an outliner.

Troubleshooting

Problem:	Probable Cause:	Solution:
The paint streaks.	There isn't enough paint on the brush.	Load more paint on your brush so it flows out and flattens, and add a little thinner to the paint to improve the flow.
The paint is full of bubbles when applied to the glass.	The paint was stirred or shaken too vigorously.	Don't shake the paints. Stir them gently before applying the paint to the glass, and avoid jabbing the paint with the brush.
Bubbles form after baking.	The paint didn't air-dry long enough before baking.	Check the label on your paints for the correct drying time; most require at least 24 hours before baking.
The whites turn brownish when baked.	The paint burned.	Use an oven thermometer to check your oven's temperature, and make sure you use the correct setting.
The paints do not withstand dishwash-ing well.	The paints have been improperly used or diluted.	Make sure that your glass surface is properly degreased, that the paints are not diluted with water, and that you followed the baking instructions.
Markers do not flow.	The markers have not been prepped.	Be patient; shake vigorously, and then press down on the tip for several seconds before beginning to paint.

Suncatchers: Working with Outliners

Creating sumptuous suncatchers to hang in your windows for a sparkling reflection of light and color is a great place to start your journey in glass painting. The small, flat surfaces are easy to work with, and the templates provided in this book make designing a cinch. I encourage you to alter the template designs to please your own artistic eye, or—better yet—create some of your own. You may want to work out your color scheme beforehand with markers or colored pencils, or simply follow mine. Suncatcher blanks (unpainted glass pieces) can be found at craft stores in a variety of shapes, but make sure to ask for glass (not plastic) ones.

Sparkling Suncatchers Demonstrated here from left to right are the black outliner, the pewter outliner (a visual imitation of the lead in stained glass), and the gold outliner.

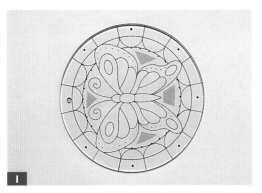

Step One Photocopy the template provided on page 12, enlarging it as necessary to fit your suncatcher. Cut a few holes around the design, and use those openings to tape the template to the back of your glass. Leave the paper around the design so you can use it to move the piece around without touching the glass.

Step Two After cleaning the glass, begin outlining your design, starting in the middle and working out toward the edges. (Do not outline the butterfly antennae or paint the dots yet; they will be added later.) At this point, you can either bake the piece or let the outlines air-dry before you begin adding the colors.

Step Three Starting at the center of the design, fill in each section with color. Avoid pressing on the outline if you haven't baked the piece yet. On the wing, swirl a little red into the yellow. Let the paint dry until it is tack-free.

Step Four Add the butterfly antennae and the dots. Let the paint dry for at least 48 hours, and then bake according to the instructions on your paints. Hang your suncatcher on a ribbon or string and enjoy!

Tips for Success with Outliners

1. Use even pressure, dragging the tube away from the paint line. Try to keep the line thin, as shown in the photo (near right). Avoid bumpy lines (far right) and very thick lines (middle); they may bubble when baked.
2. Avoid touching the glass as you paint. Keep a paper towel handy, and wipe the tip of the outliner often to keep it clean.
3. Paint the color up to the outline, but don't cover it.
4. Use enough paint so it flattens without streaks but not so much that it spills over the outline.
5. Lift out bubbles with your brush or carefully poke them with a craft knife or toothpick.
6. You may want to bake the outlines before adding color, so you can wash off mistakes without ruining your outlines.

Suncatcher Templates

Photocopy each template, enlarging or reducing as needed to fit your suncatcher.

Painted Fishbowl:
Sponging on a Curved Surface

Sponging is an easy way to cover large areas with an even, textured finish. On this fishbowl, sponging creates colorful borders and provides a soft background for the seaweed at the base. This is a comical, "cartoony" design, so consciously adopting a wobbly outline style—used by many professional cartoonists—is perfectly acceptable if you find it hard to keep a steady line over the curved surface (though once you get used to following the curve, it will get easier). Just keep in mind that the paint will have a tendency to run as you turn the bowl.

Fanciful Fishbowl Painted glass is perfect for giving the appearance that this mischievous cat is peeking in from behind the bowl. The fish is painted on the front side of the bowl, and the cat is painted on the back.

Step One Photocopy the template, adjusting the size as needed to fit your bowl. Tape the fish template to the inside of the front face of the bowl, a little to the right of center. Then cut triangles out of the edges of the cat template so that it can conform to the curved surface, and tape it to the inside of the back face of the bowl.

Step Two Clean the glass, and then outline the fish with black outliner. Outline the cat next, being careful not to touch the fish outlines. (And don't set the bowl down on the outlines; even when dry, the paint from outliners is easily dented until it has been baked!) Let the outlines dry, or bake the bowl before going to the next step.

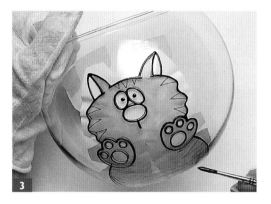

Step Three Now paint the yellow body of the cat. This is a large area, so work quickly while the paint is still wet. Don't thin the color for this section; that will tend to make the paint run down the curved bowl. Try to create as level a work surface as possible by keeping the work area pointing up. You may want to position the bowl face-up on a towel as it dries (be careful not to set it down on your outlines!), or blow-dry the paint with a hairdryer while holding the bowl in place. **(Be careful to keep the nozzle at least 6" away from the wet paint to keep the paint from scorching or being blown out of place.)** Bake the bowl again, or let the paint dry before continuing.

"Handy" Tip

I often wear lightweight cotton gloves when I'm painting on glass so I can handle the piece without leaving skin oils on the surface, which would prevent the paint from adhering. I cut the fingers out of one glove to make it easier to manipulate my brushes, but I leave a longer section of glove on my little finger; I rest my hand on that finger as I paint. Packages of these gloves can be found in photography and art supply stores.

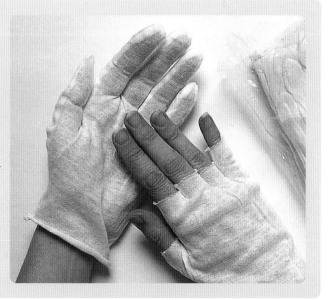

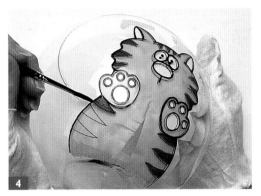

Step Four Thin some orange paint with about 1 part thinner to 7 parts paint, and paint in the stripes on the cat body. If you have not baked the yellow paint, be careful layering the orange over the yellow.

Step Five Paint the ears, nose, and paw pads with pink, and let the paint dry. If you haven't baked between colors, make only one pass with your brush over any given area to keep the underlying colors from dissolving and breaking up.

Step Six You can paint the fish with any colors you like; I used turquoise blue, green, and purple. When you're handling the bowl, be very careful not to touch or set the bowl down on the cat you have painted on the other side. Grip the bowl at the lip, and rest it on your work table, being careful to set it down on an unpainted area.

Step Seven For the base border, dip a fine-grained sponge into a generous amount of undiluted green paint (the sponge will soak the paint up quickly). Dab the paint around the base, lightening your touch where the border ends to create a soft edge. Dab a few more times over the first layer while the paint is wet to even out the finish. You can sponge over the cat if you have baked it, but don't go over it more than once if you haven't baked. **(Don't forget: You shouldn't bake a piece more than three times in total.)**

Step Eight For the top border, sponge around the top of the bowl with undiluted blue paint. Pay close attention as you paint the lip, and make sure it is properly covered with paint. You will probably need to angle the sponge into the crease just below the lip, so the area is evenly filled in with color. Leave a little unpainted space above the fish, and lighten your touch on the lower edge to create a soft line.

Step Nine Cut a small circle out of a fine-grained sponge. Dip the circle in the paint you used for the top border, and dab on three spots for air bubbles between the fish and the border. Let the paint dry. Cut out the seaweed templates, and tape them to the inside of the bowl, positioning them so they face the front and overlap the border at the bottom.

Step Ten You'll probably find it easier to paint this section if you turn the bowl upside down. Place an inverted bowl on your work surface, and prop the edge of the fishbowl on top. Begin painting the main stem of the seaweed with the purple outliner, making little dots along either side for the plants' spores.

Step Eleven Paint the leaves of the seaweed with emerald green, using the "one-stroke painting" method described on page 9. Working toward the stem, press down on the brush to make the thick part of the leaf, and lift up to taper off the leaf at the stem. Let the paint dry for at least 48 hours, and then bake. Finis!

Fishbowl Templates

Photocopy each template, enlarging or reducing as needed to fit your fishbowl.

Pasta Canister:
Merging and Blending Paints

You will love merging glass paints—it's easy to do, and the effect is gorgeous. By blending and swirling the rich glass colors together, you can create the look of real pieces of stained glass. And the color combinations and ways to combine them are endless. You won't want to limit yourself to painting veggies once you see how easy this is to do!

"Stained-Glass" Pasta Canister
This leaded-look canister is created with a combination of dark outliners and translucent paints.

Step One For narrow jars and bottles like this pasta container, it isn't always possible to tape the template to the inside. Here is a trick for keeping the template in place: Cut a piece of paper to fit the inside of the front panel. Photocopy the template to the correct size, and tape the templates to the piece of paper. You may want (or need!) to cut the letters and vegetables apart and rearrange them to fit. Then slide your assembled template into the canister, and stuff with wadded newspaper to hold the template in place.

Step Two As always, clean the outside of the glass first. Then, using the black outliner, paint the outlines, working from the top of the design to the bottom. Keep a can or box close by, the same height as the side of the canister, to rest your hand on when painting at the edges. Let the paint air-dry, or bake the canister after the outlines have dried for 48 hours. Now you're ready to fill in areas of color with interesting merges and blends.

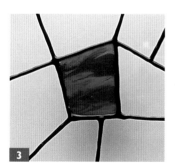

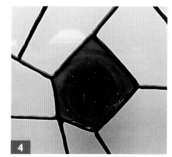

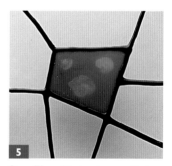

Step Three Begin a blue and purple merge by painting in stripes of blue. Working quickly so the paint does not have time to dry, fill in between the blue stripes with purple. Rinse and dry your brush, and then stroke it back and forth where the blue and purple meet. Don't overwork it, or the colors will blend too much.

Step Four For this spiral red merge, first fill in the section with the lighter red color. Then load up a clean, dry brush with the darker color of purple, and swirl it into the red while the paint is still wet. Once again, don't overwork it, or you'll get a solid purple blend instead of a swirled merge of color.

Step Five Next make a spotted pattern. To create this green-on-blue design, first fill in a section with blue. Then, while the blue is still wet, load your brush with green, and let a few drops fall into the wet blue paint. Be careful not to load the brush with too much green or the spots will overpower the background.

21

Step Six Fill in the sections on the top border with merges of color, painting each section one at a time. When choosing colors to blend or merge, bear in mind that colors near each other on the color wheel will look only subtly different, whereas colors opposite one another will create a vibrant contrast (see page 23). Once you've finished the border, move on to the letters and vegetables.

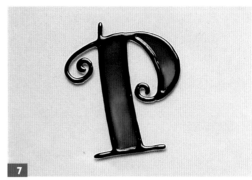

Step Seven For the letters, choose colors that don't have too much contrast, such as the blue and purple shown here. Paint a small section at a time so the paint remains wet while working with it. Begin by painting purple into the top half of each section. Using a clean, dry brush, paint blue into the bottom half. Then lightly brush back and forth between the colors to blend them.

Step Eight Fill in the body of the tomato with red, leaving two spots free of paint where you want the highlights to be. Then, with a clean, dry brush and while the red is still wet, swirl a generous amount of yellow into the spots and out into the red.

Step Nine Paint each small section of the leaf at a time. Start with yellow at the inside of each section, and then paint green at the outside with a clean, dry brush. Lightly stroke between the two colors, pulling the yellow into the green and the green into the yellow.

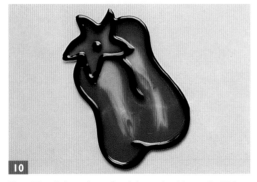

Step Ten Paint stripes of red down the sides and middle of the pepper body. Fill in between the stripes of red with yellow. Using long strokes with a clean, dry brush, pull the yellow and red into each other to blend them slightly.

Step Eleven Begin the garlic by filling it in with white. Using a few long strokes, paint purple into the underside of the garlic with a clean, dry brush, creating a shadow on the underside.

Step Twelve Paint the sections of the bottom border as you did the top, choosing whatever colors and merges you like. Let your pasta canister dry for 48 hours; then bake. Bon appétit!

The Color Wheel

This is a color wheel showing the three primary colors (yellow, blue, and red) and the secondary colors (green, purple, and orange), which are created by mixing two primaries. Colors directly opposite each other are called *complementary colors,* and they provide the most contrast when placed next to each other. Be careful when blending complementary colors; merging them is fine, but they can turn muddy when mixed together.

Pasta Canister Templates

Photocopy each template, enlarging or reducing as needed to fit your canister.

Beaded Perfume Bottle: Embellishing with Glass Beads

Colorful, glittering glass beads are the perfect complement to glass paints. The beads will bring your painted surface into three dimensions, creating sparkling facets that reflect the light and enrich the vibrant colors of the paints. It's great fun to shop for beads; there are so many gorgeous colors, interesting shapes, and beautiful designs to choose from. Just make sure the beads you buy are made of glass or crystal. Plastic beads may melt in the oven when baked!

Beautiful Beaded Bottle An array of sparkling glass beads embellish this star-filled, painted-glass perfume bottle.

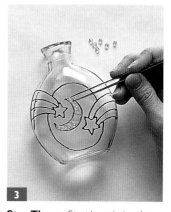

Step One   Photocopy the template, adjusting to fit your bottle, and tape the bottle to the paper (the neck will be too small to insert the design). The image may be somewhat distorted, but it will provide a rough guide for you to follow.

Step Two   Clean the glass, and outline the design with the black or dark blue outliner. If you have trouble seeing the design, try closing one eye, or draw the design freehand with the template for reference. Let it dry, or bake the outlines.

Step Three   Start by painting the moon white. When the paint is tacky dry, press clear beads into it with your fingers or a pair of tweezers. If the paint is too wet, the beads will slide; but if it's too dry, the beads won't stick. Then let the paint dry fully.

Step Four   Fill in the area around the moon with royal sapphire blended with turquoise. When the paint is tacky, place blue beads in this "sky" to represent stars. You may want to paint in small sections, adding beads as you go, so the paint won't dry before you add beads. Just be careful not to brush wet paint over the dry layer, as the wet color will dissolve the dry paint.

Step Five   Paint the stars one at a time by first filling them in with yellow paint. Then, while the paint is very wet, sprinkle on tiny beads that match the color of the paint (such as gold or yellow), and arrange them with a toothpick so they fill the area neatly. Don't wait until the paint is tacky this time, or it may become too sticky to let you move the beads around freely. Don't worry if some beads fall off the bottle as you work; you can collect them later. Then let the paint dry.

Step Six Now paint the rays one at a time. If you work slowly, add thinner to your orange paint, and then color in the rays. Using the tiniest, matching beads, sprinkle them into the paint, as you did with the stars, and arrange them with a toothpick until the ray is filled. Start at one end of the ray, and work your way to the other end. Again, let the paint dry.

Step Seven Using the gold outliner, paint dots over the outlined edge of the "sky." Be sure to keep your dots of consistent size, and space them evenly. You're not going to add beads to these dots, so let the paint dry completely.

Step Eight In this step, you will be using your clear glass paint medium as a "glue." Pour a little out in a dish or your palette, and wait until it has dried to the tacky stage. Dip the star beads in the medium one at a time, and place them around the top curve of the "sky." Then, while you wait for your bottle to dry and bake, you can go on to embellish the cork.

Step Nine First check to see how far the cork fits into the neck of the bottle, and mark that point. Using the tip of the glue bottle or a toothpick, spread a clear-drying glue over the sides of the cork, from the top edge down to the point you have marked. Sprinkle the tiniest beads over the glue, letting the extras fall off, until the glue is covered in beads. Let that section dry, and then repeat the process for the top of the cork, using a different-color bead of your choice.

Step Ten Next pick out a larger bead to use for the border, and then squirt a little of the glue onto a piece of paper. Using your fingers or a pair of tweezers, dip the beads individually in the glue, and place them evenly around the rim of the cork. Now let it dry completely, and the cork is done and ready to adorn your beautiful beaded bottle!

Painted-on "Beads"

Why not paint your own beautiful glass beads? Paint a background color first, and then draw dots and lines with the outliners for a raised design. Or merge the paints together into swirls of color. While painting, put the beads on a toothpick stuck into a piece of Styrofoam,™ and leave them there to dry. And here's a trick for baking them: I placed mine on a strand of wire, kinked to keep the beads apart and stretched between salt and pepper shakers. In fact, the shakers were newly painted and ready for baking too, so I "killed two birds with one stone"!

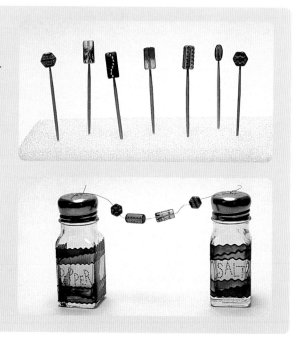

Perfume Bottle Template

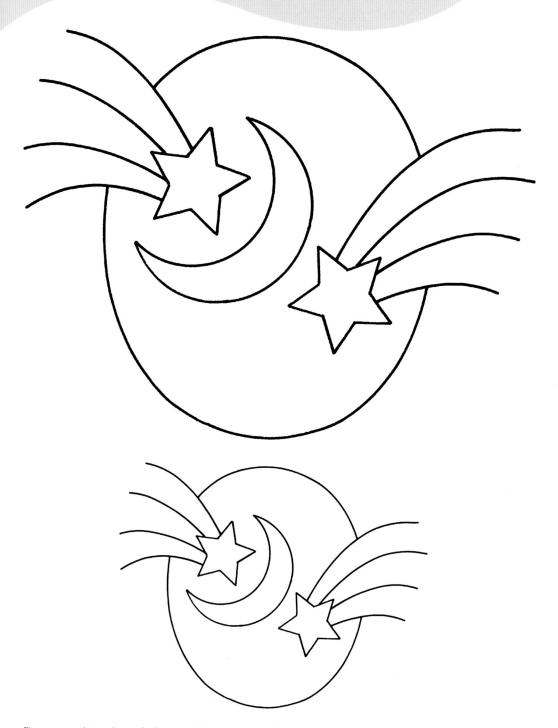

Photocopy each template, enlarging or reducing as needed to fit your bottle.

Olive Oil Bottle:
Painting on Glass Jewels

Embellishing with painted glass jewels is delightful and easy, and both the clear and the colored glass jewels are readily available at craft and import stores. Whether painted to look like olives or ladybugs, their charm is in their realistic, 3-dimensional look and the additional reflections of color and light they bring to your piece. Once you've tried it, you'll find yourself trying to think of all things roughly oval in shape that you can paint using them!

Jeweled Oil Bottle These jewel-like nuggets look beautiful all by themselves, but when painted with radiant glass paints, they're transformed into sparkling, translucent olives that look as if they will pop right off your bottle!

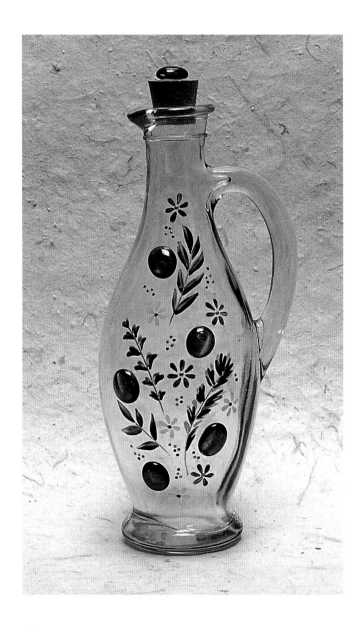

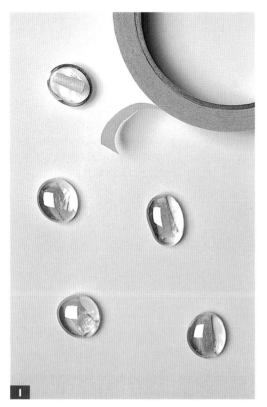

Step One This project doesn't have a template, so feel free to either copy my design or create one of your own. (Try out the design on paper first.) Then count out enough jewels for your design plus one extra for the cork. Anchor the jewels to a piece of paper with circles of masking tape. This will keep them in place while you paint.

Step Two Clean the jewels first, just as you would any other glass item you're painting. Begin by painting the tops and sides with olive green, covering the surface completely. Let the paint dry. You can dry the jewels thoroughly at this stage, or you can go on to the next step once the paint is at least tacky dry.

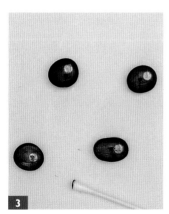

Step Three Use a wet—but not dripping—cotton swab to swirl off a round spot of paint on one end of each jewel. Keep the cotton swab upright as you swirl. If the paint is too wet, the spot will fill back in, but don't worry. Just wait a bit and swirl again with a clean swab. Let the paint dry.

Step Four Next fill in the swabbed-out spot on each jewel with red outliner to represent a pimento. Let the jewels air-dry, or dry them for 48 hours and then bake them. If you bake them now, you can glue the extra olive to the cork right away, as shown in Step Five.

Step Five Once it's been baked, glue the extra painted olive to the top of the cork with a clear-drying glue. If your bottle will be used for decoration only, you can use any all-purpose or craft glue. If you expect to use the cork frequently, you may want to use a stronger epoxy glue.

31

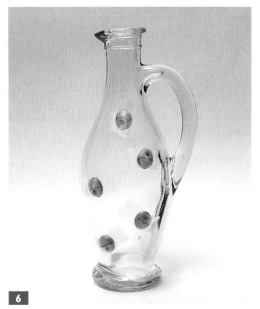

6

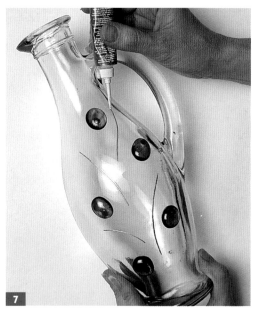

7

Step Six Pour out a little clear glass paint medium, and let it dry for a few minutes until it is tacky. It can now be used as a glue. After cleaning the bottle, apply some medium to the flat side of each olive jewel with a brush or toothpick. Place the olives on the bottle, one at a time, and anchor them in place with a strip of removable transparent tape. Be careful not to push down on the tape, as it may dent the "pimento" if you have not baked the jewels first. Let the olives dry on the bottle, and then carefully remove the tape.

Step Seven Paint some long, sweeping stems around the olives with the gold outliner, leaving room on either side of the stems for leaves according to your design. Remember, if you make a mistake or just aren't pleased with your design at any point, you can always wash off the offending paint as long as you haven't baked it yet. If you need to move any olives, apply water to the undersides with a toothpick or cotton swab, and carefully lift off the jewel. Wash off any leftover medium, and reglue the jewel where desired.

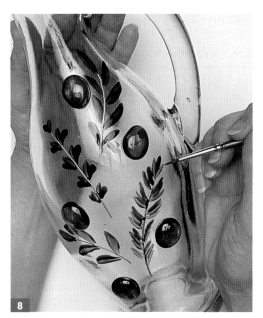

8

9

Step Eight Using leaf green and the one-stroke method used on pages 9 and 18, paint in leaves with different shapes to represent herbs such as basil, rosemary, and oregano. Let this layer of paint dry before going on.

Step Nine Next create a darker green by mixing a little black with the green color you used for the leaves. Use this color to paint a shadow on the underside of each leaf, and let the paint dry again.

32

Step Ten Now make a new mix of a little white and yellow with the leaf green, and paint a highlight on the top of each leaf. Let the paint dry so you don't smudge the leaves while you're painting the flowers.

Step Eleven In the open spaces around the herbs and olives, add some white and purple flower petals (don't paint the flower centers yet), using the one-stroke method. Again, let the paint dry.

Step Twelve Now you can add the centers to the flowers. Make a dot in the center of the white flowers with the red outliner, and paint a dot in the center of the purple flowers with the gold outliner. Then paint clusters of dots with the red, gold, and black outliners to represent spices. Wait 48 hours, and then bake. Your jeweled bottle is now ready to fill with olive oil and beautify your kitchen!

Pedestal Fruit Bowl:
Glass Painting with Markers

Everyone enjoys drawing with markers, and now you can draw on glass with them! Drawing, as you may know, affords you a different type of control than painting does. The drawing tip of a marker is uniform and stable, as opposed to the variations in paint brushes. The only "trick" to painting this fruit bowl is to loosen up your style to achieve a playful, abstract look. Be free with your lines and fills; let them flow and go where they will. Use the template as a guide, but don't be afraid to draw outside of the design. The overall look of movement and gaiety in this piece depends on the expressiveness of your drawing.

Fantasy Fruit Bowl This free, loose, and funky design is created entirely with glass paint markers.

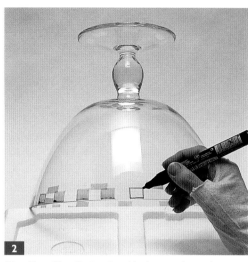

Step One To make a rough guideline for drawing the checkerboard borders at the rim and base of the bowl, cut small pieces of masking tape and place them where you can reach them easily. Then, clean your glass pedestal bowl, and measure 1/2" down from the rim and in from the edge of the base, using the pieces of masking tape to mark off the space you've measured. This way, when you draw the checkered squares, you can maintain the same general distance from edge without making a perfect line of squares. Remember: the whole idea is to make the design casual and loose, not formal and rigid.

Step Two Turn the bowl upside-down, and prop it on something to keep it from slipping, such as the piece of packing foam shown above. Start your light green marker flowing by shaking vigorously and then pressing down on the tip for several seconds. Beginning at the rim, sketch each square first, and then fill it in with even strokes. Space the squares far enough apart to allow for another square between them. As you near your starting point, gauge the number of squares that will fit the remaining space, and adjust accordingly. Turn the bowl right-side-up, and repeat the same step for the base. Let the paint dry.

Step Three Draw the alternating squares with dark green. Leave a slight gap between the squares or let them just butt, but don't overlap the edges. Let the paint dry. You may want to bake at this point to make the colored squares permanent since the next step involves layering color on top of them. However, it is quite easy to remove one square at a time with a wet cotton swab and redo it if you aren't happy with your layering. Such adjustments can even add to the hand-painted, imperfect look you are after.

Step Four Using the black marker on the dark-green squares and the blue marker on the light-green squares, draw alternating squiggles interspersed with spirals as shown. If you have not baked the bowl yet, make sure the marker is flowing well when layering colors. If it's not baked, the marker may catch on the color below and damage it. If this happens, let the paint dry and go over it again when the marker is flowing well, or remove the entire square with a wet cotton swab and redo it. Then let the paint dry.

Step Five Make several photocopies of the template page so that you have many different fruits and leaves with which to design. Cut out the individual images, leaving the spirals and squiggles for later. Tape the images to the inside of the bowl, staggering the fruit and leaves to give your design movement and interest. Tape four evenly spaced leaves to the bottom of the base.

Step Six Using a scrunched towel to prop your bowl into place, start painting one fruit at a time, moving from left to right (if you are right-handed) so that your hand can rest on the clear space ahead of you. Be careful as you work your way around that you don't place still-wet or tacky paint onto the towel. Starting with the pear, begin with the lightest color of orange for the background. Draw with long, even strokes, working quickly while the paint remains wet. Then swirl in the circular highlights with pink. Don't try to make sure the pink butts all the way to the orange. Stay loose.

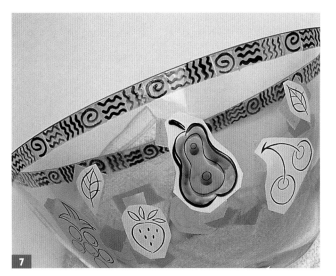

Step Seven Next draw the shadow around the perimeter of the pear with light green, again using long, even strokes. Paint one side first, and then the other side. Now let the paint dry before going on.

36

Step Eight Get the black marker flowing well. (It is important that all the colors flow easily, but it is especially critical when layering.) Add some quick, sketchy outlines around the pear, and then add the stem. If you haven't been wearing cotton gloves, you should always clean the glass in the area you are about to paint next, as all the handling you do will leave oils on the surface of the bowl.

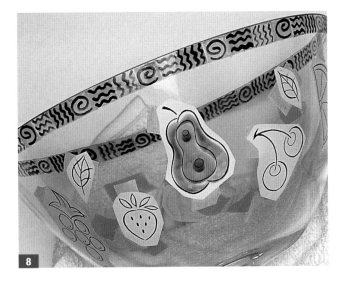

Step Nine Color in the body of the cherries with a pink marker, using side-to-side curving strokes and leaving the center under the stem clear. Then swirl a circle of red into the spot just where the stem connects to the cherry. Let the paint dry.

Step Ten Get the black marker flowing well again, and outline the cherries with loose strokes. Then draw in the double stem, and clean the glass, if needed, for the next image.

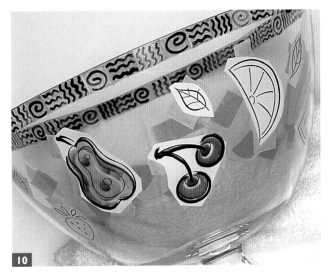

Step Eleven Color the background of the leaf with dark green marker, and let the paint dry before layering. Get the blue marker flowing well, and draw the leaf veins with quick, loose strokes. Let the paint dry.

Step Twelve Get the black marker flowing well, and outline either side of the leaf with quick, loose strokes. Clean the glass for the next image, and work your way around the bowl this way, coloring the various fruits. Refer to the photo of the finished bowl for color guidance if needed. When you're done, stand the bowl upright, and paint in the leaves at the base. Let the paint dry.

Step Thirteen You may tape in the templates of squiggles and spirals to trace, but they're so easy you probably won't need to. Draw the squiggles and spirals with markers of varying colors, filling in the open spaces on the body of the bowl. Don't fill in your design too tightly, though, or it will become crowded and look too busy. Then add pink spirals to the base between the leaves. Let the paint dry for 24 hours, and bake. Now show off your artistic talent with this exquisite bowl!

Fruit Bowl Templates

Photocopy each template, enlarging or reducing as needed to fit your bowl.

Floral-Patterned Plate:
Opaque Layering with Drybrush

There may be times when you prefer a more opaque look, rather than the transparency that glass paints normally display. I have found a way to create that look simply and easily, and the effect is that of your painted imagery floating in the clear glass. Using a drybrush technique, as you would with gouache or watercolor, you can also add a painterly, more detailed flavor to your piece. Using this method, you can paint any detailed picture, such as a landscape or a holiday scene. We'll start here with simple flowers.

Painterly Floral Plate Opaque painting and drybrush allow you to give this flowery plate its soft look and pastel coloring.

Step One Photocopy the template, adjusting the size to fit your plate. Position the center flower in the middle of the plate, and tape the template to the back. Cut along the outer ring of flowers so that the paper will follow the curve of the plate (or cut out the flowers and place them individually), and tape the template to the back of the glass. Then clean the glass.

Step Two Start by mixing only a small drop of color into white paint, as shown in the center of the palette. Mix and use one color at a time, so the paint will not dry out (here I have mixed magenta, red, purple, blue, and yellow with white). If the color won't spread well, add a little thinner. And always mix your paint with the stem of your brush to protect the bristles.

Step Three As you paint, hold the plate as level as possible. Dry each section with the hairdryer on a low setting, held at least 6" away. Paint in the background colors, one color at a time, starting with the middle flower. Then work around the edge, drying as you go (don't paint the tiny leaves along the leaf sprays yet). Let the paint dry, or bake.

Step Four Now you are ready to dry-brush. Practice on a piece of paper first, until you get the hang of it. Dip your brush into the pure color that matches the opaque background color of the section you will drybrush. Press the brush down, holding the stem upright, and wiggle the bristles apart. Quickly make short, light strokes with the splayed tips of the bristles, lifting up at the end of each stroke. Experiment until you get a feel for the technique, rinsing and drying the brush often to avoid paint buildup.

Step Five Paint a shadow on each long stem first. Then, starting in the center of each leaf and angling your brush at the outside edges, drybrush the leaves from their outer edges in toward their center veins.

Step Six Paint a center line on each leaf, and add tiny leaves to the leaf sprays with emerald or dark green paint. Use the one-stroke method described on pages 9 and 18.

Step Seven Drybrush the centers of the flowers, working from the outside in. Then drybrush the yellow leaves below the flowers.

Step Eight Drybrush the flower petals, working from the centers out. Add little strokes of paint to accent the tiny flowers and their centers.

Step Nine Paint outlines around the centers of the flowers, the petals, and anywhere else you want to define an edge. Wait 24 hours before baking your flowery creation, and then it's ready for use or display!

Floral Plate Template

Photocopy the template, enlarging or reducing as needed to fit your plate.

Wedding Flutes:
The Etched-Glass Look

Frosted glass paints offer you the ability to create an etched-glass look simply, without harsh chemicals or sand-blasting. It's as easy as sponging and one-stroke painting! The opaque, matte look of the frosted paint is a perfect foil for the shiny, transparent glass. Using white alone creates an elegant, polished pair of champagne wedding glasses. However, frosted glass paints come in the full array of colors, so don't feel you need to limit yourself to white!

Frosted Wedding Flutes
The contrast of frosted paint with clear glass endows this set of wedding glasses with an elegant, etched-glass look.

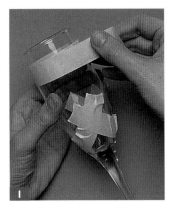

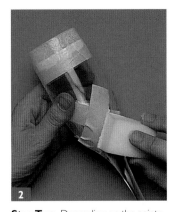

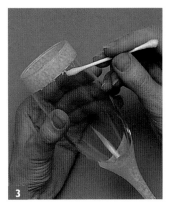

Step One Place a ring of masking tape 1/2" to 5/8" below the glass rim. Pull the tape tightly and let it fold a bit to fit. Mask above the stem with two pieces of tape, each following the curve of the glass and overlapping at the high points of the stem as shown. Press the tape firmly, and clean the glass thoroughly.

Step Two Depending on the paints you have, either use frosted white or mix the frosted medium with white. Sponge the paint on at the rim and the stem, leaving the body of the glass clear. While the paint is still wet, make a few passes with your sponge to even out the texture. Remove the masking tape, and let the paint dry.

Step Three With a moistened cotton swab, clean up any paint that bled under the tape. Be careful not to overload the swab with water, or it will drip down and mar the areas you've sponged. Also be careful not to touch the painted area of the glass, and make sure that you swipe over the ragged edges only.

Step Four Photocopy the templates to size on a dark setting so the lines will show through the white paint. Cut two holes near the center of the base template, and use those spots to tape the template to the bottom of the glass. Cut the long strip for the glass rim at the inked edges, and cut a few notches so it conforms to the curve of the glass. Tape it inside the rim.

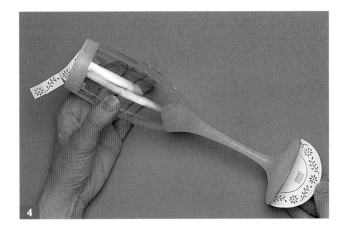

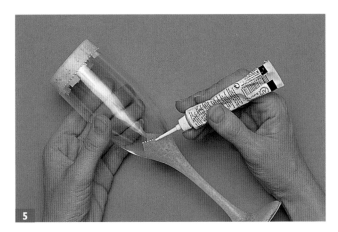

Step Five Using the white outliner, paint a series of dots along the edge of the sponged rim, the sponged stem, and the circle on the base. Try to keep the size and spacing of your dots consistent, and be careful not to touch the dots you have painted. Even when it has dried, the paint can dent and pick up fingerprints. Let the dots dry, or bake the glass.

45

Step Six Before you start to paint the details, make sure you have a strong light source so you can clearly see the template through the paint. Then, using the white outliner, trace the design along the rim and at the base, being careful to avoid touching what you have already painted. You can now remove those templates if you like. Let the paint dry, or bake the glass. Don't forget that you shouldn't bake a piece more than three times, so if you're planning to bake more than once, do it strategically!

Step Seven Tape in the template for the flower, using the curve of the sponged stem as a placement guide. If you haven't baked it yet, be careful not to disturb your dots or outlines when taping. Mix a little frosting medium with frosted white to help it flow, and paint the stem of the flower with an angled or small round brush. Hold the glass as level as possible, and steady your hand so you get a long, clean stroke. Paint the flower petals and leaves using the one-stroke method (pages 9 and 18). Let the paint dry.

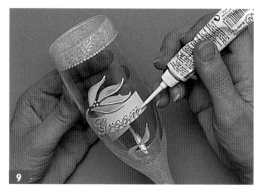

Step Eight Using the white outliner, add accents to both the flower petals and the leaves by drawing a single line along one edge of each. Then paint on three dots at the base of the petals with the outliner. Remove the template, and let the paint dry.

Step Nine Tape in the template for the lettering, centered inside the curve of the flower and parallel to the rim. Then slowly and carefully trace the letters with the white outliner. Let the paint dry for 48 hours, and bake. Your elegant flutes are now ready to present to some lucky couple!

Lettering Style

Type is an art form all by itself, and there is an amazing array of different styles available. Search for type you like on your computer, if you have one; many programs come with a variety of typestyles. You can also buy CDs of type at computer stores, ranging from conventional fonts to fun kid's stuff, and art stores carry books of type you can look at for reference.

Bride	*Bride*	*Bride*
Groom	*Groom*	*Groom*
Jan	*Rachel*	*Caitlin*
John	*Gary*	*Scott*
Mr.	*Mr.*	*Mr.*
Mrs.	*Mrs.*	*Mrs.*

Wedding Flutes Templates

Bride

Groom

Photocopy each template, enlarging or reducing as needed to fit your flutes.

Holiday Ornaments:
Painting with Applicator Bottles

Create your own hand-painted ornaments this holiday season with a quick and easy technique that covers the curved surface of a bulb like a sheet of shimmering silk. Applicator bottles allow you to spread the glass paints beautifully and thinly, producing a reflective yet transparent sheen that will set your house aglow with color. I have used one or two colors per bulb, but you may apply as many colors as you have applicator bottles.

You can find plain bulbs in boxes of a dozen at craft stores during the holiday season. You can also find applicator bottles made specifically for paints and glass paints at craft stores. Beauty supply stores carry applicator bottles as well, or you can recycle your used hair-coloring squeeze bottles, as long as you clean them out thoroughly!

Shimmering Holiday Ornaments Squirting glass paints over bulbs with squeeze bottles creates a shimmering background for the hand-painted holly, snowflake, and poinsettia details.

Step One Dilute your colors with about 1 part thinner to 7 parts color, and pour the paints into the applicator bottles. To stabilize it, place the bulb on a stick or pencil wrapped with paper. (Cover your work area with newsprint, and wear a plastic glove on the hand that will hold the bulb.) Squirt your first color over the top of the cleaned bulb, letting it run down and off the bottom. Don't cover it completely. Guide the paint with the bottle tip, and work quickly. Apply the next color while the first is still wet.

Step Two Set the bulb in a glass jar to dry. It's important to prop the bulb upright at this stage, because the paint will continue to drip and spread out as it dries. You can bake the bulb now, or wait until the paint is completely dried before continuing to the next step.

Step Three Draw the snowflakes with the white outliner, using the templates as a guide. You can either leave the bulb on the pencil while you paint, or hold it in your hand, as long as you wear a cotton glove. Even though the paint is dry, if the bulb has not been baked, it will pick up fingerprints. Before baking it, let your ornament dry for 48 hours, and then remove the supporting stick or pencil. You can clean off any paper that stuck to the paint with warm water. Then it is ready to bake.

Step Four You will need to keep your ornaments propped up while baking. I set my bulbs on metal skewers or potato bakers and place them inside another glass piece to bake. (It's especially handy to have another painted jar or bottle that is ready for baking at the same time!) After your ornaments are baked and cooled, fit the hangers on the necks, and string them with some festive holiday ribbon!

49

Step Five For this poinsettia ornament, first cover the bulb completely with iridescent medium. Make sure you stir the medium well before you use it; the flakes tend to settle at the bottom. Paint the poinsettia petals with the one-stroke method (pages 9 and 18). Add dots to the center of the flower with gold outliner, and draw the conifer branches with green outliner.

Step Six For the holly ornament, first squirt on layers of yellow and white for the background. Then paint on the holly leaves with a small brush or outliner. Add the holly berries by dotting them on with a red outliner.

Using Reference Photos

References for designs are plentiful and easy to come by. Magazines, newspapers, books, cards—all provide an endless supply of imagery. Art and craft stores sell books with designs of all kinds, and they can also be found on the Internet. Keep a journal of designs and images you come across that attract you. Then, when you're ready to paint, you'll have your own, handpicked source of inspiration.

Holiday Ornaments Templates

Photocopy each template, enlarging or reducing as needed to fit your ornaments.

Whimsical Mirror: Stenciling

The fanciful, dreamy quality of this mirror is achieved by repeating and layering the images in an asymmetrical, almost childlike fashion, coaxing the beholder to meditate on the heartfelt, hand-written message. And stenciling makes it simple to create and repeat images that give this piece its hand-drawn look and innocent character. You can also make your own stencils to match the mood of your favorite saying: stars and moons may grace a message about dreams, flowers and teacups for friendship, or roses and hearts for love. This is a great gift for someone you wish to inspire with your personal words of encouragement—or for yourself to enjoy!

Message Mirror This whimsical mirror owes its charm to the stenciled images and the golden accents drawn with outliner.

Step One Photocopy the stencils from this book, or sketch your own, but do include an appropriately sized oval for the center of your mirror to use as a mask for your border. Transfer your stencils onto card stock (unless your machine can copy directly onto card stock). Use a light table, or hold the papers up to a sunlit window to help you see what to trace. Then cut the stencils out of the card stock with a utility knife. (You will be using the oval itself, though, not the oval hole.)

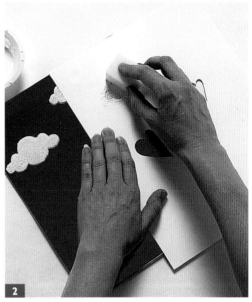

Step Two Clean the mirror as you would any glass item. Then, starting with the cloud, hold the stencil in place and sponge paint over it until the image is filled. Don't press too hard, and don't shove paint underneath the edges; use a firm but light hand. Move around the mirror and sponge as many clouds as you like, letting some of the clouds run off the edge of the mirror. Make sure you wait for one cloud to dry before sponging the next one so as not to disturb the paint, or use a hairdryer to speed up the drying time.

Step Three Next sponge over one of the heart stencils, using the method you used for the clouds. Move all around the mirror, randomly overlapping both the clouds and the hearts wherever you like.

Step Four Sponge the second heart stencil around the mirror using a different shade or a different color than you used for the first heart stencil. Overlap some of the other hearts and clouds. Let the paint dry.

Step Five Cut two squares out of the oval template, and center the oval on the mirror, leaving slightly more mirror showing at the bottom. Tape the template through the two holes, and sponge the background color around the border. Use the corner of the sponge to paint around the hearts and clouds, but you do not need to be precise; the design is meant to be loose and soft. Let this layer dry.

Step Six Choose a darker color than the border color—in this example, I used royal blue—and randomly sponge in spots of color over the lighter background to give the border a mottled look. Let the paint dry. If you want more protection before you add the lettering (in case you need to wash off your mistakes), you should bake the mirror before going on.

Step Seven Write your message at the bottom using an outliner. I used gold, but white or pewter would work as well. Practice writing your message in pencil on a sheet of paper first, so you have some idea of how much room it will take before you start writing on the mirror.

Step Eight Using a variety of colored outliners, add tiny stars (or asterisks) and hearts of different sizes and proportions around the border and over the stenciled images. Let the paint dry for 48 hours, then bake, and your message mirror is complete!

Whimsical Mirror Templates

Photocopy each template, enlarging or reducing as needed to fit your mirror.

Colorful Candlesticks: Doing a Flat Wash

The flat wash technique is a wonderful method of covering an area easily and evenly, creating a shiny, lustrous surface. As long as you work with the paint while it remains wet, you can cover even very large areas with a flat wash of glass paint. For this project, the bases and tops of the candlestick holders are painted with the flat wash technique, and the color-coordinated stems are painted with a small round brush for a confetti-like effect. You can choose any color scheme you like, but the unrestricted use of color on these candlestick holders makes them a sure-fire match with almost any decor.

Candlestick Holders A colorful array of small brush strokes on the stems of these candlestick holders sets off the solid bases and tops, painted with a flat wash.

Step One Cover your work area with newsprint, and clean the glass. Thin your base color (I used blue) with about 1 part thinner to 4 to 8 parts color. If you're using a light color such as orange or yellow, use less thinner so the color stays strong. Hold the glass upright, and stroke downward only with a wide, flat brush, rotating the glass until the base is covered and letting the paint drip off the bottom. When the dripping has slowed, brush off any pools of paint at the bottom edges. Set the holder down in the upright position to dry completely, and then repeat this process for the top.

Step Two Using wet cotton swabs, clean up any ragged edges from drips or any place where you overpainted into the rings above the base and below the top. Once all the edges are clean, you can bake the glass or let it air-dry. If you do decide to bake, you might want to paint the top and base of the other candlestick holder now, so you can bake both candlesticks at the same time.

Step Three Paint the rings with a contrasting color—here I used green. Add a small amount of thinner to your mix to retard the drying time. You'll want the paint to still be wet when you have completed the ring and joined the point where you started. If the paint has dried, don't try to brush over it; just paint right up to the edge without overlapping it. Let the paint dry.

Step Four Starting with one of the base colors and a small round brush, paint small strokes of undiluted color around the stem at a 45° angle. Don't apply the paint too thickly, or it will run and pool. Keep your strokes spaced far enough apart to allow you to add several other colors. If you are handling the glass at the top or base, remember to wear gloves, or you will leave fingerprints. Let the paint dry.

Step Five Now start adding more strokes of any colors you choose, keeping your lines at a 45° angle. You can butt the colors up against one another, but it's nice to leave some clear glass so the strokes from the other side show through, creating a colorful contrast. Let the paint dry, and then bake. You'll have your choice of candles for these holders, since just about any color will look great!

57

Peacock Vase:
Using an Angled Brush

Iridescent glass paint medium is like a jar of crushed opals that change color as they catch the light at different angles; one minute you see a painted surface of azure blue and emerald green, and the next minute you see the paint light up with a shimmering glow. Iridescent medium is also very versatile. You can create a range of effects, from translucent to opaque, depending on how thickly you apply it. And you can add the medium to any color, so just one little jar will give you virtually a whole new set of paints to work with.

For a project like this one, where you want to paint long, thin lines, you may want to purchase an angled brush. It can hold enough paint to last the stroke, and it keeps its shape while you draw out the line. It will help you make an easy job of these peacock feathers.

Peacock Feather Vase
Peacock feathers, which themselves are opalescent, are a perfect subject for the glistening
iridescent glass paints.

Step One Photocopy as many feather templates as you need to fit around your vase. In this example, I used four, alternating the templates provided in this book. Roughly cut out the feather templates, and tape them to the inside of the vase. Depending on the shape of your vase, you may have to cut notches in the paper templates so they conform to the curve of the vase. Then clean the glass.

Step Two Mix about 1 part iridescent medium to 2 to 6 parts color, keeping in mind that the medium will lighten the color to a degree. Begin by painting the gold area—mix yellow with a tiny drop of brown, along with the iridescent medium. Paint thickly while holding the vase as level as possible. To speed up the drying process, use a hairdryer while holding the vase in place, keeping the nozzle at least 6" away from the painted glass.

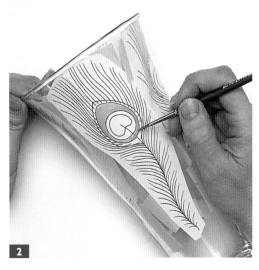

Step Three Next mix turquoise blue with the iridescent medium, and paint the area of the feather just inside the gold ring. Again, dry it with a hairdryer. Although here I demonstrate painting on only one feather, you should move around the vase, painting in the appropriate section on each feather with the color you've mixed, and drying as you go. Remember not to touch the areas you have painted—even if they're dry—to avoid leaving fingerprints.

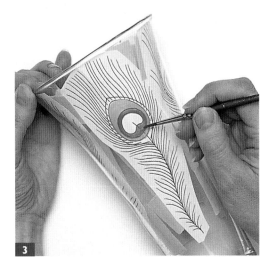

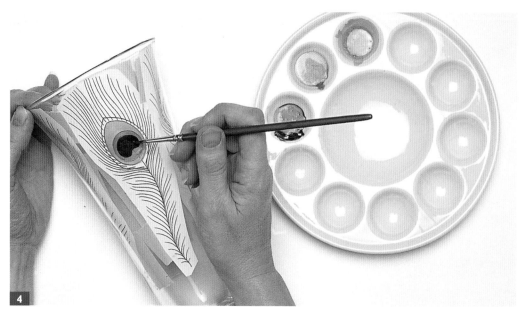

Step Four Next mix royal blue with the iridescent medium. To make sure the royal blue in the center of the feather stays dark enough to contrast with the surrounding turquoise, add less medium than you used with the turquoise. Paint the centers of the feathers, drying as you go.

Step Five Mix a light green using green, yellow, and the iridescent medium. Paint a thick outline of green around the areas of gold in each feather, drying as you go. Try to butt the green up to the gold, but don't worry if the colors overlap a little.

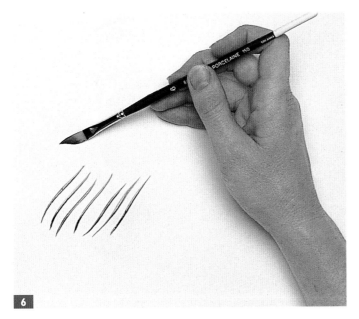

Step Six For the wispy outer edges of the feathers, mix a deep green with the iridescent medium. Practice making strokes with the angled brush on paper before you try it on the vase. Although I hold the brush sideways for my practice strokes, I hold the brush upright when I'm painting on glass.

Step Seven Paint the lines on the feathers with the green you've mixed, using the template only as a guide. Don't try to follow the template exactly; be loose and let your lines flow freely. Allow your strokes to glide along the angled brush bristles, turning the brush slightly to curve the line, and paint right up to the lip of the vase. Don't worry if you paint onto or over the lip; you can clean up the stray paint later. When you have finished painting the lines, let the paint dry, or use a hairdryer to speed things along.

Step Eight Mix turquoise blue with the iridescent medium. Using the angled brush again, paint shorter blue lines between the green ones on the outer edges of the feathers. Use a hairdryer, or let the lines air-dry completely.

Step Nine Clean up any stray paint marks from the lip of the vase rim with wet cotton swabs. The next step is to add accents with an outliner, so you may want to bake the vase at this stage, in case you need to clean off any mistakes you make with the outliner.

Step Ten Using the gold outliner, draw a stem down the center of each peacock feather. Let the paint dry for 48 hours, and then bake. You are now ready to arrange fresh, dried, or silk flowers in your beautiful, iridescent, hand-painted vase!

Peacock Vase Templates

Photocopy each template, enlarging or reducing as needed to fit your vase.

More Great Glass Painting Ideas: The Next Step

Once you've begun this creative journey in glass painting and discovered how beautifully plain glass transforms into dazzling works of art, you'll want to explore even further. And the possibilities are endless. From old jam jars to panes of window glass—you'll never run out of new and interesting things to paint. Shopping for glass is exciting once you've become familiar with what these radiant paints and a little imagination can do. You may find that the shape of the glass will often suggest the design. Keep that journal of ideas and images. Let yourself flourish as an artist, with no judgments or expectations; just paint and enjoy the play of sparkling color on glass.

One good way to develop your drawing skills is to trace. Get a pad of tracing paper and some soft pencils. Find some images you like, such as flowers or animals. Place them under a sheet of tracing paper, and trace the salient features. This exercise will help you develop a familiarity with the lines of a rose or the muscular shape of a tiger. You'll find this to be an excellent practice that will build your confidence and skill as an artist.

Remember, there is no right or wrong in art. Art is subjective. No one can tell you what to like, you just like what you like! Your own color combinations are perfect, and your own particular style is unique. So don't let anything hold you back, and, above all, have fun painting glass!

Ideas for Inspiration Now take the techniques you've learned in this book, and create your own painted glass treasures!

64